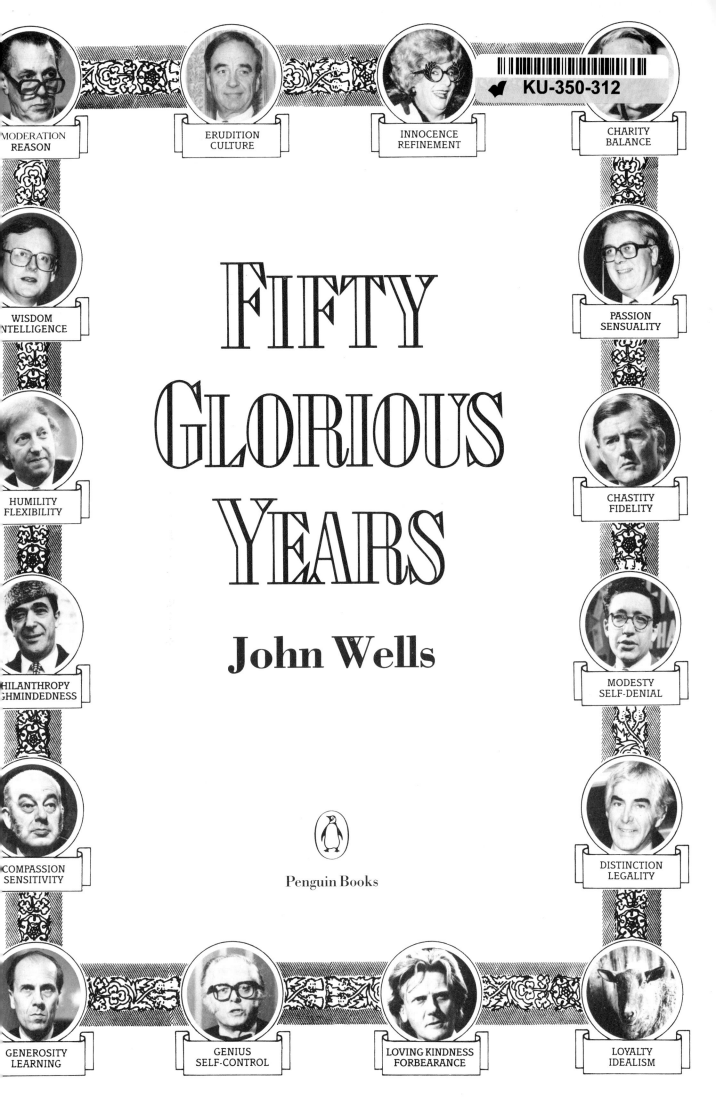

MODERATION
REASON

ERUDITION
CULTURE

INNOCENCE
REFINEMENT

CHARITY
BALANCE

KU-350-312

WISDOM
INTELLIGENCE

PASSION
SENSUALITY

HUMILITY
FLEXIBILITY

CHASTITY
FIDELITY

PHILANTHROPY
HIGHMINDEDNESS

MODESTY
SELF-DENIAL

COMPASSION
SENSITIVITY

DISTINCTION
LEGALITY

GENEROSITY
LEARNING

GENIUS
SELF-CONTROL

LOVING KINDNESS
FORBEARANCE

LOYALTY
IDEALISM

FIFTY GLORIOUS YEARS

John Wells

Penguin Books

The author and publishers wish to express their gratitude to the simple artisans and craftspersons whose contribution to this festive volume, offered for the most part almost entirely gratis at the chance to share in paying homage to Our Leader, has been almost literally invaluable. To Ms. Linda Martin, for extricating the manuscript; to Russell Ash Esquire, for his patience, forbearance and flashes of delightful insight in an Editorial capacity; Mademoiselle Jenny de Gex for seeking out literally millions of photographs from which the present obsequious selection has been made; to Bernard Higton Esquire for 'laying out' the Heroine and her attendant Heroes pictured within, and to Keith Richens for the very wonderful and inspiring portrait of Margaret Hilda Thatcher on the front cover. The Prince Consort Denis was dressed on the Right by Morris Angel & Son Ltd, and photographed in the studio of Michael Busselle, not of Ottawa.

Penguin Books Ltd, Harmondsworth, Middlesex, England
Penguin Books, 40 West 23rd Street, New York,
New York 10010, U.S.A.
Penguin Books Australia Ltd, Ringwood, Victoria, Australia
Penguin Books Canada Ltd, 2801 John Street, Markham,
Ontario, Canada L3R 1B4
Penguin Books (N.Z.) Ltd, 182-190 Wairau Road,
Auckland 10, New Zealand

First published 1984
Published in association with Pavilion Books Ltd
Copyright © John Wells, 1984
All rights reserved
Typesetting by Front Page Graphics
Made and printed in Great Britain by William Clowes Ltd,
Beccles and London

Picture acknowledgements:

BBC Hulton Picture Library
Camera Press
J. de Gex
Mary Evans Picture Library
Fine Art Photographs
Sally & Richard Greenhill
John Hillelson Agency
Alan Hutchison Library
Illustrated London News
Photo Library

Keystone Press (incorporating
Central Press and Fox Photos)
The Kobal Collection
Mansell Collection
Network/Chris Davies
Network/John Sturrock
Popperfoto
Rex Features
Syndication International
John Topham Picture Library

Special illustrations by Tony Escott
Photomontages by Denis Hawkins
Photoprinting by Geoff Goode Photographics
Artwork by Andrew Greenow

A purely symbolic role: The Right Honourable Neil Kinnock (r),
By the Grace of God Defender of The Faith & Leader of the Labour Party, seen here
relaxing with Mrs Kinnock (l) in their unpretentious Welsh home.

In the olden days, the Leader of the Labour or 'Work' Party exercised real power in the land. If you read your history books you will even see pictures of Labour Prime Ministers, all of them carrying out acts of great derring-do and gallantry, coming to the aid of the poor and needy, defending the weak against the strong, and in a word ruling the country.

Today this is obviously no longer the case, and it's easy enough to see the Leadership of the Labour Party as an outmoded, meaningless relic of the past, for all its colourful pageantry and quaint ritual, with no relevance for this day and age. But let's just consider for a moment whether that is a fair assessment of an institution that delights foreign visitors and adds so much to the rich tapestry of our British tradition.

When I stand up in the House of Commons as Leader of Her Majesty's Opposition, I have a great many words to say, some of them very long and complicated ones. Often, to people listening to those words broadcast on the wireless or reading them printed in the newspaper, they must seem well-nigh incomprehensible. In many instances I actually find it very hard to understand what I am saying myself. So "why talk for the sake of talking?" I am often asked. In answering that question I try to explain to people about the sheer beauty of the English language, particularly when it is pronounced with the irresistible lilt and melody of a Welsh accent, and also about the wonder, the infinite fascination of the sound of the human voice, particularly my own.

But why make these long and largely incomprehensible speeches 'opposing' the will of Our Leader Margaret Hilda Thatcher? Why waste the nation's valuable time filing in through the 'Noes' lobby when the outcome is inevitably going to be another mighty and triumphant victory for reason and common sense as embodied in Tory legislation?

The answer I think lies in the miracle of the British Constitution. It's all a question of balance. Where would Cain have been without Abel? David without Goliath – though that particular contest, in Thatcherite terms, went badly wrong? You can't, in a word, have a victor without a vanquished. Without organised opposition here at home that can be symbolically 'duffed over' by Our Iron Lady in the same way as foreign opponents like General Galtieri or President Mitterand abroad, how would the people of Britain be made permanently aware, day after day, Question Time after Question Time, of the invincible power and pugnacity of Our Great Leader?

One other question crops up from time to time about my constitutional position, whether it be flat on my back after one of Our Leader's world-famed uppercuts, or merely hanging on the ropes waiting for it. "Why me? Why not someone else?" Indeed it is a question I have many times asked myself.

The answer? If it wasn't me, *it would be someone else.* No names, no pack-drill, but the fact that I fulfil this role of 'blocking' other less suitable Leaders of Her Majesty's Opposition as I sit here on the pinnacle of the symbolic constitutional pyramid is a real sense of comfort to me.

Neil K.

A PIECE OF CAKE

Leading Lady, Governess, Mother Superior to us all, Margaret Hilda Thatcher has given new meaning to the words of her ancestor Marie Antoinette de Bourbon (1755 – 1793) "Let them eat cake".

Of course they can eat cake,
IF THEY DESERVE IT . . .

But like the raggle-taggle of work-shy, politically-motivated militants Mrs Bourbon was talking about in the olden days,

THEY usually don't deserve any cake at all.

THEY challenge Our Leader's authority, in the Falklands, on the picket lines, in Council Chambers, even in the Cabinet.

THEY pigheadedly refuse to 'get on their bikes', even to 'stand on their own feet' – preferring to loll about at the public's expense in the Chronic Ward at their local hospital. Bloody-minded old widows who can't be bothered to raise the necessary capital to buy their own council house. 'Students', provincial ballet-dancers, Left-wing vicars.

It is to Margaret Hilda Thatcher's everlasting credit that she has had the courage to identify the enemy, to re-draw the battle-lines. Traditional British class warfare, once threatened with extinction, is flourishing as never before. Old war-cries, long-stifled, are heard again: "Me first!" "F*ck you, Arthur, I'm all right!"

For too long, under a succession of jelly-kneed 'fair shares for all' merchants of all political persuasions, the National Cake has been sliced paper-thin. Now, inspired by the vision of that big fat slice Our Leader holds out to the deserving few, 'self-made' English men and women, canny Scots and their 'wee wifies' from North of the Border, beady-eyed Taffs from the valleys and their coal-black Mammies, Orange men and Orange women from Ulster have flocked to her azure skirts.

The cry has gone out: "Help yourselves!" – and they have. People with nails in their boots who mean to come out on top of the heap. People we can all admire. People like the Crown Prince Mark, Margaret Hilda's natural heir.*

In the pages that follow we pay homage to Our Leader and the Victorian Values that have been re-established in her glorious reign. Fifty Glorious Years of Our Warrior Queen. Our Iron Lady. Our Modern Britannia.

*Now living in exile in the United States.

NOT FROM THE HAUNTS OF PRIVILEGE...

Born of poor but hardworking parents in the market town of Grantham in Lincolnshire, Margaret Hilda Thatcher *née* Roberts was stung to the quick when Moscow stooge Denis Healey of the now purely symbolic British Labour Party called her "La Pasionaria of Privilege".

Not only did she bear no physical resemblance to the overweight flamenco dancer in question; she had begun life, she insisted, with few material advantages. She did not even know how to play the castanets.

In Our Leader's autobiography *You Have To Laugh!* (World Humor Library, $3.25), Margaret Hilda Thatcher describes having to crack the ice in the family's unpretentious brick 'three-seater' lavatory at the bottom of the garden to release her father, 'Economical Alf' Roberts, whose frugal way of life rejected any such luxuries as electrically-heated lavatory seats as 'wet'.

His daughter Margaret Hilda inherited the same fearless approach as she assumed the throne.

Our Leader's birthplace:
a quiet backstreet in old Grantham.

From her father too, Our Leader learned th full-blooded Victorian values of basic economic Why waste money on over-manning and stropp employees when you can do the job yourself? It is lesson that Margaret Hilda Thatcher has vigorous applied both to the economy as a whole and to th Cabinet in particular.

'Economical Alf' also instilled into Our Leader th importance of 'keeping the punters happy', an Margaret Hilda still remembers her father leavir family meals in the shop – traditionally taken over th counter to avoid wasting time – to perform th amusing 'yodelling clog-dancer' routine that inspire Margaret Hilda's own dazzling comic performance both on the hustings and at Question Time in th House of Commons.

Enemies of Our Leader and her triumpha economic policies have asked why it is th 'Economical Alf', for all his wisdom, omitted to stam the family name of Roberts on a great chain of grocei stores akin to Sainsbury's or Patel's Kash 'n Kurri. The fail to read the message of hope that blazes from o Alf's kindly eyes: he was creating not an Empire but a Empress!

'Economical Alf' Roberts, Our Leader's father:
"If you wants a job done, do it yourself".

DECENT PEOPLE, WITH DECENT VALUES...

For all Alf's economies and their at times very straitened circumstances, the family never gave in to squalor.

For Mrs Roberts, Our Leader's worthy mother, it was a duty to keep up appearances. One room in the house, her own bedroom, remained untouched by the harsh realities of cut-throat competition, inviolate against the intrusion of potato sacks, sides of bacon, paraffin tins and boxes of broken biscuits that make up the grocer's stock-in-trade.

Here Mrs Roberts, like the great hostesses of pre-Revolutionary France, gave a Thursday afternoon *salon* and *thé dansant* that set the infant Margaret Hilda's eyes afire and toes a-tapping to the infectious rhythms of Ol' Bananaroll Ingrams and his Jolly Coons, Sidney 'Mr Red Hot Poker' Torch, or Yehudi Menuhin and his Washboard Rascals.

Le Tout Grantham it seemed, was there, rubbing shoulders with regulars from London, Paris and New York. It might be Marcel Proust, demonstrating the then fashionable 'Shimmy', Arthur Askey talking about Existentialism, or the exiled King Haile Selassie of Ethiopia performing questionable conjuring tricks. Whoever it was it gave the young Margaret Hilda a feeling for Culture that was to lend power to her elbow when she took her pruning hook and set to work.

Mrs Roberts 'at home'.

happy inspiration of immobilising the brakes of Gresley's 'Pacific' Flying Scotsman as it steamed at 65 mph into Grantham Junction?

But it was not all fun. If she played hard, she worked hard too. Reorganising the timetable at her infants' school so that richer children who could afford it might have the freedom to choose particular teachers and particular times of day best suited to their other social commitments. Improving morale by arranging stone-throwing matches with 'foreign-looking' or 'common' boys from rival schools. And always making grown-ups feel absolutely at their ease.

THE AGE OF INNOCENCE

Sophisticated though the young Margaret Hilda must have been, trained up in the careful thriftiness preached by her father and brought to an early flowering in the hothouse of her mother's drawing-room above the shop, the golden tales still spun by old men at the Grantham Athenaeum Pool and Snooker Club dwell most upon her innocence and playfulness.

Time to dream – of a New Britain?

Who else but the infant Margaret Hilda Roberts, one day to be Our Leader, would have scattered marbles on the stairs at the Labour-controlled Darby and Joan Home for Indigent Social Workers? Who else but Margaret Hilda have laced the Grantham Liberal Party's Christmas Punch with Epsom Salts? Who else, in a madcap scheme to 'punish' the LNER for running late, have had the

Teaching an old dog a few new tricks –
T.S. Eliot (l) looks on as the young Margaret Hilda Roberts 'cleans out' Marcel Proust (r). Both were regular guests at her mother's Thursday afternoon *salons*.

"A RIGHT LITTLE BOBBY-DAZZLER"

Few schoolgirls in history, with the possible exceptions of Joan of Arc and Zola Budd, can have equalled the dazzling achievements of Our Leader Margaret Hilda Thatcher in her time at Grantham's Lady Constance Narkover Academy for the Daughters of Gentlefolk. She knew that sacrifices had been made to send her there – her father 'Economical Alf' had scrimped and saved, and there had even been some much-regretted curtailment of the imported blue movies hitherto enjoyed by the intellectuals at Mrs Roberts' afternoon *salons*: Margaret Hilda was determined that such sacrifices should not have been made in vain.

So it was that the trim, elfin, bright-eyed Margaret Hilda of twelve summers threw herself with characteristic energy into a programme of work that would have reduced, and indeed did reduce, many other girls to hysteria and despair. As the youngest Head of School since 'Wee' Georgie Wood in 1817, she immediately carried off the Vivienne Squeamish Marathon Debating Mace, the Dame Millicent String Spear for Tribal Dancing, the Mavis Hotter Hat and Club for Unarmed Combat, the Cyril Hotter Machine Gun for Armed Combat, the Ethel Slavering Gold, Silver, Bronze, Lead and Putty Dumbells for Bullying On and Off, the Gertrude Hat Award for Grievous Bodily Harm, and most of the School Armoury.

Thus equipped, Margaret Hilda launched a frontal attack on staff, structure and institutions, inflicting savage cuts, many of them in highly sensitive areas, inspired by refreshingly original view of education that was to b confirmed many years later when she and her husban Denis came to assess the value of sending the Crow Prince Mark to Harrow. And all this in her first term.

The same characteristic pattern repeated itself a Somerville College Oxford. Making do with a fev minutes' sleep a night, the future Leader amazed th grey-beard dons at her own college and male teacher throughout the University with her intellectual brilliance breathtaking beauty and biting wit that could reduc lecture theatres to a storm-tossed sea of helpless mirth.

Sadly, her plans to put the University back on its feet b selling off half the colleges for commercial use as massag establishments and luxury hotels ran into the entrenche opposition of purblind reactionaries. Her schemes t instal check-out desks at the University's libraries, makin a realistic charge for the use of books, like those t introduce free-enterprise ticketing for lectures an University sports fixtures were also blocked.

Nonetheless she succeeded, as always, in stirring u strange and savage passions. When, still a researc chemist, she burst into the national consciousness wit her astonishing discoveries, it seemed the world was he oyster. But other achievements in widely different field of human endeavour were to follow swift upon thei heels, leaving her public thrilled and exhilarated (se pages 10-11).

"I'm not lucky, I deserved them":
Margaret Hilda Thatcher, still a junior girl, proudly displays a few of her awards.

Strict discipline was the order of the day at the Lady Constance Narkover School for the Daughters of Gentlefolk, where Our Leader Margaret Hilda Thatcher spent her formative years. A contemporary photograph shows the scripture teacher, Mr Purvis, explaining the Parable of the Good Samaritan.

Healthy minds, healthy bodies: oil painting of the school's founder, Lady Constance Narkover (l) as Captain of Staff Gym Team. She was a fervent believer in the educational value of PT.

Another Madame Curie: In one short week of 'doodling in the lab' Margaret Hilda Roberts had invented radium, split the atom and discovered penicillin growing on a pair of her father's cast-off combinations. She is seen here in more sombre mood, brooding on a sample at the Combined Services Urological Research Laboratory, Papworth.

THRASHING THE WORLD

Our Leader's buttocks claw at the upholstery as she coaxes a few more crucial revolutions out of her Three Thousand Horsepower Facel-Vega Hatchback Variant to clip seven minutes off the world record at Brooklands.

Suspense: Margaret Hilda Thatcher scrambles back to safety after having to 'get out and get under' her Rolls-Bentley Seventeen-Litre Hatchback Convertible during the Cross-Latvia Scramble. From l to r: Lady Cunard, Theda Bara, Boy George, Ex-King Zog of Albania, Mr 'Bud' Flanagan and Margaret Hilda Thatcher.

A 'thirties superwoman: Margaret H Thatcher leaves the radio mast of the Em State Building in New York to establish a first in free-fall parachute jumping – witho 'chute!

She flies through the air: realising that her undercarriage had collapsed shortly before landing at Luton International Airport, Margaret Hilda Thatcher has the presence of mind to 'hitch a lift' from Amy Johnson, leaving her co-pilot in the rear seat, the young Willie Whitelaw, to splash down near Watford.

You can't win 'em all!! Our Leader takes a spill in the Winter Olympics Tobaggan event down the slopes of Mount Everest

In secret training near Chorley Wood for the triple somersault and corkscrew backflip that won her the cherished Golden Vulture at the Zagreb Olympics.

"Owzat?!" Wicket-keeper Mother Teresa of Calcutta appeals in vain as Margaret Hilda Thatcher (r) nears her third century in the Vatican Test at Old Trafford.

Look, no hands! Margaret Hilda Thatcher establishes another world record with seven hundred and thirty five hours non-stop motorcycling on the 'wall of death' at the Finchley Bowl.

Whoops! A sticky moment in the Harrods Food Halls Round The World Air Race as Margaret Hilda Thatcher makes an unscheduled landing in the Thames Estuary.

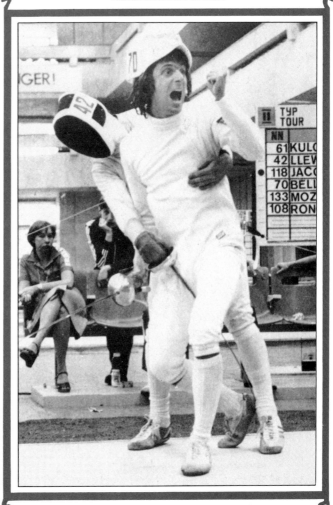

Touché!! Spoilt brat Alphonse de Noailles-Périgord (r), reigning French foil champion, quibbles over a point as Margaret Hilda Thatcher (in mask, l) thrusts home her advantage.

RENAISSANCE LADY

For a young woman in the inter-war years endowed with such a bewildering variety of gifts and so effortless a mastery of so many apparently conflicting disciplines, the choice of a career was by no means easy. In her letters at the time to Albert Einstein – later published in five volumes by the World Humor Library under the title *Dear Walrus* – she toys with thoughts of the ballet, a career in primitive brain surgery, even with nuclear physics as applied to abstract art.

Neither these intellectual preoccupations nor her astonishing feats in the realm of international sport however shielded her from the gossip columnists, eager for news of romance. Though her future consort Denis was already as she put it "on a back burner", simmering away in anticipation of their eventual betrothal in the late 'forties, she was unable to deny persistent rumours that linked her name romantically with that of Edward, Prince of Wales, and she professed herself to be "jolly relieved, quite frankly", when the then King Edward VIII married Mrs Simpson on the rebound.

While she brooded on her eventual destiny, it was to her favourite hobby of motor-racing that she was to turn for relaxation. Isolated in the bucket seat of a mighty racing car, thundering through space at speeds often in

"All right for a bit of slap and tickle": Margaret Hilda's judgement of the future King Edward VIII. His handicap bore no comparison with that of her eventual consort Denis.

Denis: "on a back burner"

excess of a hundred and fifty miles an hour, she could read, think and ponder on the fundamental truths of what was to become her political philosophy. It was the race track that taught her the wisdom of 'no U-turns' that she was later to apply with such irresistible logic to the guidance of the British economy. The way must be cleared of lame ducks, do-gooders, and other human detritus. Foot down, full speed ahead, and no time-consuming debates about the ultimate objective.

Make way for the Leader!

However white-hot the intellectual energy that forged her political beliefs, the Iron Lady remained at heart an artist, always sensitive to the promptings of the creative spirit, of the soul. Even during thirty-second stopovers in the pits, as oil-smeared mechanics swarmed about her, she would pull out a scrap of manuscript paper and jot down ideas for arias and orchestral interludes that were to become *Moses e Lulu*, her first performed opera.

The opera, set in Biblical times, tells the story of Moses, a poor politician, struggling to liberate the people of Israel from the Union stranglehold imposed by the Pharoah which he believes is sapping Egypt's competitive ability in the Ancient World. Moses falls in love with Lulu, daughter of Gideon, the successful head of a small paint-making corporation whose father had stumbled on a chemical substance known as Arsenite and founded the family's fortune by marketing it as a sheep-dip and hair-restorer. Moses determines to woo her. Disguised as Sherbet Seller, he infiltrates Gideon's encampment by night, and sings the still popular *Hear my Song (Rigoletto) drifting o'er the Blue Lagoon*. The work's triumphant reception at Covent Garden won Our Leader Margaret Hilda the praise of both Igor Stravinsky and the young Bernard Levin.

Margaret Hilda Thatcher's, first opera, *Moses e Lulu*. She is seen here rehearsing with Arnold Capacci (Counter Tenor), Efrem Wunderlich (Baritone) Gordon Mountjoy (Mouth-organ Continuo) and Enzio Vespucci (Bass).

THE VOICE OF SANITY

Margaret Hilda Thatcher (l) is seen here with Field Marshal Goering (r) putting the final touches to a non-aggression pact that could have prevented the Second World War.

As an internationally acclaimed athlete, sportswoman, political philosopher and three times winner of the Nobel Prize for Literature, Margaret Hilda Thatcher found herself, very much against her will, drawn into the world of international diplomacy. Politicians as disparate as Mussolini and Stalin beat a path to the door of her parents' shop in Grantham to seek her advice, to draw strength from a woman many years their junior, to learn firmness in the conduct of government. But even at so early a stage in her career, Margaret Hilda was never one to suffer fools gladly, as the spindly Indian pacifist Mahatma Ghandi discovered to his cost; he was sent away with a flea in his ear.

Sensing that Europe was once again drifting inexorably into war, Margaret Hilda seized the initiative to draw up plans for a European non-aggression pact that in many ways foreshadowed the present-day EEC, but with a more sensible balance of power. In return for a partial sacrifice of sovereignty which would allow a German sausage motif to be superimposed on the British national flag, Great Britain would go foward, together with Germany and Italy to play a leading role in the Community, with a treaty formula designed to curb the rapacity of the French farmer once and for all.

While in no way entirely endorsing all aspects of the German Government's stance on home affairs, Our Leader foresaw the economic advantages to Europe of a long-drawn-out conflict between Japan and the United States, who would be encouraged by HMG's 'Misinformation Service' to carry out massive pattern-bombing raids with conventional and nuclear weapons on each other's territories, thus paving the way for a post-war scenario in which British Fish 'n Chip Shops, together with German Bierkellers and Italian Spaghetti Houses would march across a ruined America much as Colonel Sanders' Finger Licking Chicken Establishments now stride across our own dear homeland. Only the obtuseness of Neville Chamberlain stood between Our Leader and European World Domination.

ANOTHER FINE MESS...

As 'wet' governments in Austria, Czechoslovakia and Poland increasingly provoked the German government with quibbles about the exact nature of an initially German-dominated but united Europe, Margaret Hilda watched powerless. For all her efforts, war broke out.

With a woman in charge, as Our Leader has since demonstrated in the Falklands, victory would have been ours in a matter of weeks. Instead the nation turned to a poor second best, Winston Churchill. While professing even today boundless admiration for someone she still remembers as a "charming escort", Margaret Hilda Thatcher must have found it galling indeed to write Churchill's speeches, cover up for his innumerable gaffes, and, in less sober moments, prop him up against the wall of a studio in Broadcasting House as she impersonated his sibilant growl for the listening millions.

Hostile commentators tried to discern some 'U-turn' in the Leader's attitude as she abandoned her efforts for peace to throw herself body and soul into the war effort. Their lack of patriotism did not remain unnoticed, or unpunished.

Margaret Hilda Thatcher (l) good-naturedly warns that in his inebriate condition Winston Churchill (centre) may well press the trigger of the Tommy gun he is holding for the benefit of photographers. Seconds later her warning proved correct, and Private Eccles (r) received painful wounds in the left foot.

A DAMN GOOD WAR

A sticky moment: captured by the Germans while engaged on a one-woman mission to kill Hitler, Margaret Hilda poses for press cameras before giving the Gestapo a piece of her mind.

Frustrated by the limitations of her job as Chief Political Adviser to the War Leader, Margaret Hilda Thatcher volunteered for active service, and after a gruelling course at the Womens Royal Army Corps' 'Deathshead' Divisional Headquarters at Abinger, was parachuted into Occupied Germany with the mission of assassinating the German Chancellor. In this she was only partially successful. Falling into enemy hands when her parachute became entangled in a chair-o-plane roundabout on the outskirts of Potsdam, she was taken prisoner and went through seven hours of interrogation, after which her captors came out with their hands in the air.

Like St Paul preaching in prison, Our Leader left the Gestapo in no doubt about their shortcomings in terms of scruffy turnout, lack of discipline and generally catastrophic inefficiency. Returning to a favourite theme, she outlined in glowing terms the advantages they would discover in having both the Gestapo and the even more slipshod and ill-disciplined Waffen SS run by a woman. Declining the joint role herself, she nonetheless applauded the appointment of Grete 'the White Barrage Balloon of Luneburg' Mödling, whose blitzkrieg-style

Blighty here we come! Margaret Hilda, Head of the Camp Escape Committee, can just be seen at the back of this happy group crowded aboard an exact reproduction of a 1937 Mercedes-Benz Tourer, made in Schloss Falkenstein entirely from milk bottle tops and cardboard boxes from Red Cross parcels. The 'engine noise' was provided by a home-made gramophone in the boot, and motive power came from three members of the Escape Committee lying prone under the bonnet pedalling with their teeth. Photograph by the Secretary of the Camp Photographic Society. (They were unfortunately recaptured some minutes after this picture was taken, charged with driving on the wrong side of the road.)

intervention in the so-called Battle of the Bulge came within an ace of turning the fortunes of war.

Margaret Hilda herself withdrew at her own request to the impenetrable dungeons of the dreaded Schloss Falkenstein, from whose top security block, she escaped no fewer than sixteen times.

WHERE THERE'S A WILL...

Nothing, it seemed was beyond the ingenuity of Margaret Hilda Thatcher and her fellow prisoners of war. Driven by an iron determination to get back to Blighty and have another crack at Jerry, they forged passports, dug tunnels and even built a light aeroplane, made from matchsticks and back-numbers of the *Burlington Magazine* from the Camp library, and powered by a heart pacemaker obtained from the Sanatorium.

Perhaps the most audacious escape attempt was carried out under the very noses of the German High Command. Visiting Schloss Falkenstein to see a production of Margaret Hilda's *Moses e Lulu* performed by the Camp Operatic and Dramatic Society, they little realised as they handed in their uniforms and decorations at the box office in exchange for the bedouin robes and head-dresses required for audience participation scenes, that they were playing into the hands of the escape committee. During the first act a gramophone record of the opera was put onto the turntable of a radiogram in the middle of the stage, and while the audience allowed

Don't forget the diver! A fellow-Wren gives Our Leader-to-be (l) a 'good luck' kiss as she sets off to attach limpet mines to the hulls of German cruisers, destroyers, battleships and aircraft carriers, sinking over forty million tons of shipping.

themselves to be moved by the power of the music, the cast and orchestra 'did a bunk' with both their uniforms and transport.

They had reckoned without the vigilance of a musically-educated guard at the main gate. When they told him they had found the opera "boring", and were leaving early, his suspicions were immediately aroused, and moved to test the validity of Margaret Hilda's waxed moustache, he tweaked it off, exposing her ruse.

It was the seventeenth and successful attempt, via a scheduled Lufthansa flight from Berlin's Tempelhof Airfield to Gatwick, that enabled Margaret Hilda Thatcher to resume her war effort, single-handedly bringing about the collapse of the Axis Powers in 1945.

Wizard prang! Margaret Hilda Thatcher poses for photographers on the cockpit of the supercharged seventeen thousand horsepower Spitfire-Hurricane Hatchback in which she brought down the remainder of the Luftwaffe, a truly remarkable score of kills chalked up on the fuselage.

THE WILDERNESS YEARS

Under the brutal and repressive regimes of Attlee, Churchill, Eden, Gaitskell, Wilson, Home, Heath and Callaghan, Our Leader found herself condemned to twenty-five long years in the political wilderness. Unlike de Gaulle in France, who filled in the time smoking cigarettes, mooning about Colombey les Deux Eglises or skipping in the back garden, Margaret Hilda Thatcher refused to waste a moment. She knew her day of destiny would come, and until then she meant to live life to the full, cramming every second with activity.

'Getting on her bike' in no uncertain terms, Margaret Hilda Thatcher found job after job, revelling in the rich multiplicity of opportunities for innovation, reform, and the 'tuning up' of organisations in which she found herself. It was from this rich reservoir of business, social and cultural experience, of having been thrown into close contact with people of all kinds and from every level of society, that Margaret Hilda Thatcher was to draw the magnanimity and love of her fellow citizens so evident when she came to power.

Restaurant Critic, *Grantham Echo*.

Golden Disc Award for 'Strangling Mr Shore'.

Royal Academy Prize for *Portrait of an Unknown Man*.

Restaurant Critic, *The Lancet*.

Restaurant Critic, *Healthfood Today*.

Catering Manageress, *Al-Ahram* Social Club, Cairo.

Grave amid scenes of general rejoicing, Margaret Hilda Thatcher is universally acclaimed as the first woman leader of the Tory party.

POWER BEYOND OUR WILDEST DREAMS

With the election of Margaret Hilda Thatcher as Leader of the Conservative and Unionist Party, British politics underwent the most violent change it had known since the beginning of the Ice Age.

Male dominance, both in the Party and in Parliament, had received a decisive blow. Immediately Our Leader was hailed throughout the land by jubilant crowds, clamouring for an end to the old divisive two-party system, and demanding, as soon as it was practicable, the establishment of a one-party state.

Even at the time of her first democratic election to supreme power, Our Leader still hesitated to take so revolutionary a step. But events soon forced her, much against her will, to put the constitution on a more realistic footing, and with her second 'landslide' victory in the Commons, to become Lady Protector of a fully Tory State.

> "It changed our lives."
> A triumph, too, for ordinary people: as the Brown family of Surbiton saw it, "nothing would ever be the same again".

CLEANSING THE STABLES

Nothing would have pleased Our Leader more than to share power with the defeated remnants of the old political parties – Labour, Liberal, even the renegade Labour supporters who had rallied to the sleazy banner of the Limehouse Gang of Four.

It soon became clear that such elements were not prepared to co-operate. By their attempts to interrupt Our Leader, to contradict her in public, even to thwart her will, they showed themselves for the contemptible enemies of their country that they were.

By allowing the Opposition Parties to operate within colourful 'reservations' in which they could practice their traditional war-dances and age-old rituals, Our Leader gave the dissidents the opportunity to act within the rule of law.

Those who refused were crushed without remorse.

The dramatic arrest of David Owen, ringleader of the revolutionary 'Gang of Four'. Together with three other desperadoes, he had plotted in Limehouse to overthrow the benevolent leadership of Margaret Hilda Thatcher.

He tried to destroy the Upper Chamber. Like Van der Lubbe in the notorious Reichstag Fire trial, this fanatic, believed by some to be of unsound mind and in the pay of the Socialists, attempted to destroy our democratic institutions. It was Our Leader's duty to declare the one-party state in order to protect them.

No disguise could save him: this degenerate, David Steel, seen here at the time of his arrest during a Neil Kinnock Look-alike Competition.

Liberal decadence: this remarkable photograph, taken by a member of Our Leader's crack SAS division who succeeded in infiltrating the insurgents' headquarters, shows cigar-smoking maniac Steel encouraging a female desperado to mock the forces of law and order at a fund-raising 'beano.'

A NEW AGE DAWNS

With the appointment of the Saatchi Brothers to the key job of interpreting Our Leader's policies to her people, a new age of understanding and co-operation dawned. Since the robuster days of the eighteenth century, the concept of 'buying' and 'selling' political power, of spending substantial sums of money to secure one's election, had somehow fallen into disrepute. Now, with characteristic vigour and directness, the daughter of the Grantham grocer re-established the notion as a central plank in her platform. She was in the business of persuading people, and she could afford the best persuaders in the business.

With a firm that sells Procter & Gamble's disposable nappies to Belgium, Avis Rent-a-Car to the French and Japanese television sets to Siam, Margaret Hilda Thatcher knew she was in good company. She meant to become a 'brand' name, and a brand name of record-breaking endurance and 'shelf-life'.

But there was never any question of 'brainwashing' the public. It was purely and simply an exercise in persuading the consumer to look at political phenomena in a new way.

Take unemployment. When Margaret Hilda Thatcher came to power unemployment was thought of as

Luigi (l) and Alberto Saatchi (r):
The Appliance of Science.

As if by magic, Margaret Hilda Thatcher transforms a liability into an asset. 'Unemployment, once a stigma under Labour . . .

somehow the fault of Central Government. A gloomy condition. In one dazzling campaign the Saatchi Brothers turned it into a fact of life. No one's fault. It was there. She determined to make the best of it. Fewer people with pay-packets to spend – lower inflation. Fewer jobs – less lip from the Unions. Even a touch of nostalgia – it was just like the 'thirties again!

. . . becomes respectable. Unemployed, yes. But are they downhearted? No! The workless millions learn to take it in their stride!

CRY HAVOC!

It sprang from a desperate search for some means of increasing the Government's popularity and distracting an unhappy, electorate from inflation and growing unemployment at home

General Galtieri's publicity consultants Argi y Bargi Publicidad, suggested he seize the offshore 'Malvinas' Islands. What they overlooked was that these islands had already been seized several times before by various colonial powers, and most recently by Great Britain. They were occupied by staunch loyalists, who despite repeated efforts by Her Majesty's Government to dislodge them, clung to the Union Jack.

In the circumstances, Our Leader Margaret Hilda Thatcher's patience was rapidly exhausted. Spurning the well-meant interference of the American negotiator, Earl Haig, she let slip the British Lion. After years of liberal pussy-footing in the cage of democracy, the lion bounded out at our Britannia's command to maul the enemy.

In marshalling her legions and sending them forth, an invincible armada, to cleanse the British Falkland Islands of foul enemy infestation, Our Leader Margaret Hilda Thatcher flung off the humble mantle of the mortal politician and revealed herself in her true nature, radiant and transformed – a Goddess of War.

Britain declares war on Argentina: The Nation responds to Our Leader's clarion call to arms.

As in more heroic days, the peaceable British lion (above) responds to Our Leader's summons (left) to roar defiance at the invading 'Argies'.

Senor Oswaldo O'Hagan (centre) Creative Head of Argi y Bargi Publicidad, Public Relations Consultants to General Galtieri, plans the campaign at a meeting with senior account executives.

y operation. The recapture of the Falklands was
[...]te to the planning and foresight of Our Leader,
[...]ret Hilda Thatcher. Here War Minister Nott, at
[...]r suggestion, carries out a last-minute check.

[...]gmatic, conservative-minded community: The
[...]nders struggle to contain their enthusiasm as
'our boys' battle back to victory.

Rejoice! Captain 'Rollo' Prune of *Amethyst* storms ashore on South Georgia to
overwhelm superior Argentinian forces.

Victory: British forces enter Stanley. The Islanders' home is safe.

Surprised among looted art treasures: former Minister of Culture Stevas.

Toppled at a stroke: mystic Heath 'sees stars'.

Aristocrat Gilmour after questioning.

Plotters unmasked: Heath confers with deposed War Minister Pym at the time of their trial.

A purer party: Our Leader meditates on the purge in the monetarist shrine.

A PURGE WITHIN THE PARTY

Strengthened by the resounding defeat of a South American Republic, Our Leader turned to purify the Tory Party, to purge it of those elements dedicated to dissent and disaffection.

Known as the 'Wets', these evil and self-seeking men, owing allegiance to the dangerous and explosive Edward Heath, were mercilessly exposed and expelled.

The way was open for a new era of creative co-operation among Government Ministers, loyal to Our Leader.

MORE POWER TO HER ARM

Margaret Hilda Thatcher was now ready to introduce her policies pure and unadulterated by 'wet' elements in the works. Number Ten Downing Street moved into top gear at last, a humming power house, a dynamo for change.

erved by a Cabinet of loyal Ministers, each
n expert in his own field, Our Leader
onducts the business of governing the
country.

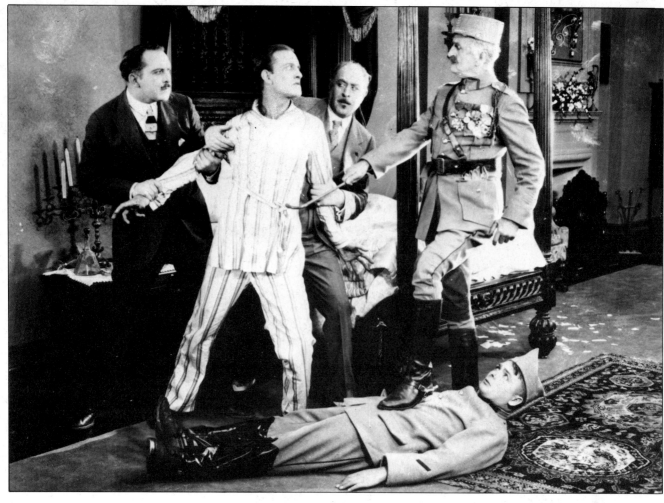

A vile allegation: former Party Organisation Chief Cecil Parkinson is accused of beastliness after the planting of false evidence by anti-Government forces.

THE YEAR OF THE LONG BANANA SKINS

Desperate in the aftermath of Our Leader's crushing final victory, anti-Government forces turned to a new and insidious campaign of smears and innuendo, fabricating any scandal, however unlikely, that might embarrass the leadership.

First victim of this infamous plan to undermine the triumphant spread of full Thatcherism was the Leader's trusted adjutant, Cecil Parkinson, accused by the crypto-Communist daily, *The Times,* of moral unclean-ness. Despite the transparent innocence of this stainless Tory pioneer, he was hounded from office.

Within weeks the Reds had struck again. This time they succeeded in diverting telegrams from the British island of Grenada, where Communist infiltrators had temporarily seized power, so that instead of being delivered to Whitehall they arrived at a glue factory in North London. As a result Our Leader was deprived of another opportunity to deploy her invincible Falklands task force and the operation of restoring freedom to the Island in the Sun was left to a raggle-taggle of drugged American servicemen.

No piece of filth, it seemed, was beneath the consideration of these terrorists of the media. It was suggested, and by some even believed, that Defence Minister Heseltine had been 'caught with his trousers down' when cruise missiles landed at Greenham Common without his knowledge. That Foreign Minister Geoffrey Howe had lost his from the window of an express train when they had become infested with bees. That he had destroyed another pair by pouring hot coffee into his own lap on an aeroplane bound for Athens.

In such an atmosphere of rumour and alarm, it nonetheless shocked decent Tories everywhere when these vermin turned their attention on Margaret Hilda Thatcher's natural heir, the distinguished thinker and philanthropist, Mark Thatcher, alleging that he had deviated from the stern path of public service.

Our Leader never faltered...

Mastermind Lord 'Willie' Whitelaw in thoughtful mood as he broods on the damage done by anti-Government smears.

TAKING ON THE BULLY-BOYS

A tougher line with the TUC: a delegation from the National Union of Railwaymen finds Margaret Hilda Thatcher in no mood for joking.

Instead, Margaret Hilda Thatcher set out to tackle the power of the Union bosses. For too long, British captains of industry and their dynamic managers had seen quiet afternoons on the golf course ruined again and again by work-shy louts making trouble on the shop floor, at the coal face or down sewers. The so-called workers must be made to understand who made the money in this country. Faced with the threat of a life frittered away on the scrapheap of unemployment, the truculent hobbledehoys and rabblerousers of the Trades Unions Congress began to see sense.

In Europe, too, the self-seeking foreigner was brought to heel. At the British Leader's approach, Hun and Frenchman alike would soon learn to quail at the appearance of Our Leader.

A new sense of respect: European councillors respond with caution to Our Leader's overtures on Britain's budget contributions.

All smiles: General Takashi Ishihara (r) jokes with pressmen as British Trade and Industry Minister Norman Tebbit (l) signs an unconditional surrender agreement.

A new spirit in the inner cities.

A hundred-thousand welcomes...

With the progress of privatisation, all kinds of exclusively British institutions were now open to the foreign investor.

During the 'thirties and 'forties of the present century, real resistance developed in the British Isles to the idea of German or Japanese firms setting up in this country and making use of British labour. Now, thanks to the foresight of Our Leader and her belief in international capitalism, we were ready to welcome friends from abroad with open arms.

...To a new-look Britain

"Old England is a Garden . . ." the old song says.

Now, under Our Leader's wise economic measures was rapidly becoming one.

Like any garden, it needs pruning. Under Our Lead guidance, Chancellor Lawson was doing just that.

Cutting everything right back.

Look round you! Everywhere you will see Our Lead hand!

Mr Asahi Banzai (centre) talks to British 'coolies' at the giant Japanese railway-building works at Changi, Tyne and Wear, about the introduction of compulsory PT and Emperor-worship before 'clocking in' at five a.m.

Squandering the Government's annual allocation to the Arts Council in one flamboyant gesture, Culture Minister Lord Gowrie (l) brings entertainment to the citizens of Barnsley.

The New Look: Savile Row goes punk.

Chancellor Lawson: being cruel to be kind.

Cheers: Local Young Conservatives celebrate the privatisation of an eventide home for the elderly, now reopened under private management as 'Wrinklies' Disco.'

BBC Economics Correspondent Dominic Harrod studies the Chancellor's latest proposals.

Wonder: Arab building contractors greet Our Leader in Oman.

Adoration: French housewives gasp in awe at Our Leader's natural chic.

T HER FEET

Delight: Margaret Hilda in appreciative mood as she inspects
comfort rooms in Tokyo with Premier Yamaha.

A meeting of minds: Papuan Monetarists turn out in force to
applaud Our Leader's moral stance.

A steadying influence: the Consort Denis as always at the
elbow when support is needed.

Public gravity: Elizabeth Mountbatten-Windsor (r) takes it on the chin as she learns from head waiter Ram Banerjee that there will be a half-hour wait in the bar as her table at the 'Memories of Empire' curry house has been given to Margaret Hilda Thatcher.

Private gaiety: alone together, as in this charming snapshot taken during 'charades' after tea at Chequers, the two women are bosom chums.

Women's Realm

Much curiosity has been aroused, both at home and abroad, by the phenomenon of a country governed, both symbolically and in fact, by two women. Surely the real ruler, commentators have suggested, must be irritated by a shrill, rather self-opinionated interloper, a person of conviction verging on obstinacy, used to getting her own way in all things.

On the contrary: Margaret Hilda Thatcher finds the Queen "a delightful little woman".

As a civil servant in a highly sensitive position, Elizabeth Mountbatten-Windsor is of course forbidden from joining a union or expressing her own opinion in public. Nonetheless Our Leader has praised her fine speaking voice, and is on record as saying that when it comes to reading a script she has written, Mrs Mountbatten-Windsor has a great deal to teach Sir Geoffrey Howe.

"Not up to Denis": on a rare occasion when his wife Elizabeth is unable to stand in for Our Leader, Philip Mountbatten-Windsor has the privilege of squiring Margaret Hilda Thatcher. Though not a patch on her own husband, Our Leader has confessed to finding Greek-born Mr Mountbatten-Windsor "really very good value". As always, Insp. Jim Callaghan keeps a weather eye open for danger.

SUPER POP-UP & PULL-OUT SOUVENIR PROGRAMME

Produced by Penis Thatcher Novelties in Association with
Picarda Flybynite Greetings Cards of Deal (Abu Dhabi) Ltd

ERRATUM

Due to the utter bone-headed bloody mindedness of
the Trotskyite trouble-makers who have infiltrated
Mr Picarda's cutting and gluing works in Guatemala,
some of the very ingenious "pop-up" features of my
celebratory "pop-up and pull-out" programme may be
found on delivery not to be entirely functional. Steps
are even now being taken to deal with the culprits.

A word about this lavish pop-up pull-out souvenir programme of events, specially devised and written for the occasion by the Prince Consort, HSH Denis.

Dear Friends,

In devising this unique, full-colour souvenir programme with the assistance of my good friend Mr Maurice Picarda of Flybynite Greetings Cards of Deal (Abu Dhabi) Ltd, I am particularly prond of the high standard of pronting made available by the most up to dite compuserised printong processes, and of the ingenious 'Pull Out – Push Back In' facility which allows the programme to be reinserted in the main binding after use.

Literature, in my own view, even literature of the most colourful kind used to promote package tours and mail order products, is very much an acquired taste, and I trust that these charming little surprises, popping up as they do on the following pages, will beckon the weary reader onward like a large drink in a dry land.

Endless enjoyment, I am sure, will be derived from operating the little levers, causing Margaret's mouth (p. 33) to widen in an enchanting smile, Oswald de Catford (p. 37) to shin down the family tree and embrace his descendant, and Auberon 'Four-Eyes' Dempster-Waugh (p. 41) to produce a small slide trombone from his clothing and play, I am assured by the manufacturers, a few bars of the National Anthem. Those wishing to manipulate the Boy Mark and who have not already done so, should get weaving with Tab B on the opposite page.

The many thousands of intricate moving elements which enable the relevant parts to pop up in such an amusing and entertaining way are all made by hand, and this in itself, I am glad to say, has provided work for a great many unemployed, largely South American *Cretinos,* whose hen-coop style workshops it has been by privilege to visit in the company of their enlightened North American employers.

POPPING IT UP

Take the part carefully between the finger and thumb as indicated and push vigorously towards the spine. The thousands of intricate bits and pieces inside will then be brought into play to produce a truly astonishing errect. This process may be repeated as often as desired, though great care should be taken to ensure that the moving parts do not become frayed through over use.

HSH MARGARET HILDA THATCHER IN THE THRONE ROOM AT THE FAMILY'S HOME IN FLOOD STREET, CHELSEA. THE PRINCE CONSORT DENIS (L) AND THE PRINCESS CAROL.

A UNITED FAMILY

My wife Margaret has always drawn great strength and support from her family. Looking at ourselves objectively, as we are encouraged to do in this democratic day and age, I find it hard to imagine a son, a daughter or a husband better suited to her aims and ideals.

Our boy Mark, now alas living in exile in the United States, seems to me to embody all that is best in Conservative youth. To have his own company, as he himself confessed to one interviewer, was "the Holy Grail that he pursued with tunnel vision": he began Monteagle Marketing, as he told another journalist "with absolutely nothing", and setting aside my own modest fortune this is entirely true. Certainly he has nothing in the way of intellectual advantages.

Our daughter Carol, too, with her keen interest in the media and avowed disinclination to matrimonial entanglements, bodies forth those Victorian values on which my wife Margaret so delightfully harps.

In describing myself as a rock, a symbol of unteetering stability on which Margaret can fall back in any emergency, I feel the biographers have paid me no less than is my due. The fact that I have been in the far-flung corners of the world on such occasions as the birth of the twins and Margaret's election to the Tory leadership in no way lessens the fact that she relies on me to be wherever I am at such junctures.

THOUGH LIVING IN EXILE IN THE UNITED STATES THE CROWN PRINCE MARK CONTINUES TO HOLD HIGH THE BANNER OF ENTERPRISE AND INITIATIVE.

ORDER OF EVENTS

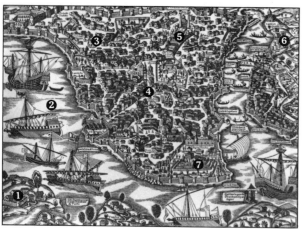

KEY

1 The Cat And Hamster
2 The Inebriate Newt
3 The Merry Leper
4 The Waggonload Of Monkeys
5 The Frog And Loincloth
6 The Arthur Scargill
7 The Bee And Surgical Support

0600 Procession Route to be cleared by The Rt Hon E. Heath as Lady Godiva.

0630 Cosmetic Battalion (Saatchi & Saatchi's Own) Set Decorators' Division to paint and hose down Procession Route prior to Principal Photography.

0645 Fifty thousand Elegant Extras (Agency HM Prisons Plc) debus at Assembly Points under armed guard (HM Securicor Forces Plc) to draw bowler hats, pin-stripe suits, Union Jacks, placards proclaiming Fifty Glorious Years.

0700 A. Scargill, K. Livingstone, Gen. Galtieri, etc to report to Wardrobe Supervisor for fitting with leg-irons, shackles, manacles, prior to move off.

0800 Breakfast for World Press Corps to be provided intravenously by NHS Plc (Methylated Spirits Division) in Royal Denis Hall.

0845 The Prince Consort Denis, supported by the Rt Hon Major W.H.S. Jump and Mr Maurice Picarda, will be accompanied to the North Door of the Cat & Hamster. Helicopter gunships and snipers of Metropolitan Police Plc stand by, Sound and Cameras Ready.

0900 Procession leaves Downing Street.

1030 Mass Rally in newly-privatised Kensington Gardens, site of multi-storey Gardens Development, to watch ceremonial storming of former Iranian Embassy by units of the SAS – 'Maggie's Mad Buggers'.

1200 March Past by Three Million Unemployed (Maggie Thatcher's Own), Units of Monetarist Youth, Class War Veterans' Organisations, Marching Band of GCHQ Cheltenham, Prisoners in Chains.

1245 The Prince Consort Denis, supported by the Rt Hon Major W.H.S. Jump and Mr Maurice Picarda, will be accompanied to the East Door of the Cat & Hamster.

1300 Luncheon.

1500 Flypast by Cruise Missiles of the USAF. *

1530 Mass Rally in newly-privatised Hyde Park, site of multi-storey Hyde Park Development, for Old Shag Heavy Tar Plc Gladiatorial Games: Fifty Strong Union Leaders to be matched with Tory-picked Gladiators and Wild Beasts, in the Gracious Presence of HSH Margaret Hilda Thatcher.

1630 The Prince Consort Denis, supported by the Rt Hon Major W.H.S. Jump and Mr Maurice Picarda, will be accompanied to the South Door of the Cat & Hamster.

1745 Grand River Pageant on newly-privatised River Thames, site of Thames Industrial Complex Plc with Armed Units of the Metropolitan Police Gay Provocation Plc assaulting GLCHQ County Hall.

1900 Dancing in newly-privatised streets, admission £500 plus VAT.

2000 Champagne Dinner at newly-privatised Buckingham Palace Hotel Plc.

2300 HSH Margaret Hilda Thatcher appears on Balcony to distribute traditional 'Maggie's Ha'pence' to Unemployed from red-hot shovel.

2400 Grand Firework Display by Units of the Irish Republican Army, Gaddafi's Formation Dancers, etc.

0300 The Prince Consort Denis, supported by The Rt Hon Major W.H.S. Jump and Mr Maurice Picarda, will be ejected from the West Door of the Cat & Hamster.

*This timing is subject to USAF confirmation.

THE PROCESSION

FIRST TANK
Pink Knocker Extraordinary, Master J.S. 'Boy' Gummer
Croydon Young Conservatives (Maggie's Musical Imps Plc)
The Editor of the *Daily Mail*
Mr Bernard Levin and Emu

SECOND TANK
His Grace Sir Kenneth Newman, Metropolitan Police Plc
'Flasher' Runcie, Church of England Plc
His Excellency the Ayatollah Khomeini Plc
Mr James Savile, OM

THIRD 'THINK' TANK
Sir Keith Joseph, Minister of Education Plc
Male Nurse Alfred 'Bonecrusher' McGurk

FIRST BICYCLE
His Grace Norman 'Darth Vadar' Tebbit

SECOND BICYCLE
Mrs Tebbit

THIRD BICYCLE
Mr Sidney Mott, Bikaway Hire Plc

THE CORPS DIPLOMATIQUE
Sir Gervase Lorent de Nosegay
Herr Gramophon von Trapp
Mrs Vegetable Spig III
His Benevolence Ali 'Concrete Bernous' Wazir, Libyan Charge
D'Affaires

THE ARMED FORCE
General Guy Clavering Motors DSO and Cuts (Retd)
BEARING ON A CUSHION THE HISTORIC KEY TO THE

NUCLEAR DETERRENT, SURRENDERED AT THE TEMPLE
BAR TO

THE UNITED STATES COMMANDANT
Hiram B. Floorpolish IV

A FLOAT DEPICTING 'THE BAD OLD DAYS'

Cinderella	Mrs Philip Mountbatten-Windsor
Baron Hardup	Lord Wilson of Falkender
Brokers' Men	Mr Roland Rat
	Mr Philip Mountbatten-Windsor
Ugly Sisters	Mr Michael Mouse
	Mr Charles 'Big Ears' Mountbatten-Windsor

A FLOAT DEPICTING 'THE NEW AGE'

Sexual Interest	Dame Rebecca Weidenfeld (Mezzo-Soprano)
Joan Bull	Mr Boy George
Britannia	The Princess Carol
The Seven Dwarves	Mr Engelbert Humperdink
	Mr 'Honest Edward' Du Cann

THE PRESS CORPS
PROCEEDING BACKWARDS ON ALL FOURS UNDER THE
DIRECTION OF THE LORD LUIGI SAATCHI, KEEPER OF THE
REPTILES

TORY WOMEN FOR VIOLENCE
'Battling Bessie' Throat
Lady Olga Maitland

HSH MARGARET HILDA THATCHER
ATTENDED BY HER MINISTERS IN THE COSTUME OF
WOODLAND FAIRIES, HARNESSED TO HER ARMOURED
TROOP CARRIER WITH GARLANDS OF WILD FLOWERS

PRISONERS IN CHAINS

ARNULF OF SYDENHAM
(2,000,053-1,999,906 BC)

HELEN BANDYKNEES
(d. 2,000,004 BC)

GASPARD OF CHICAGO
(359-296 BC)

MILLICENT THYNGE
(342-296 BC)

ATTILA THE HUN
(d. 453)

'WINNIE' VISIGOTH-ROBERTS
(862-957)

MARGARET THE SILENT
(1321-1378)

IVAN THE TERRIBLE
(1530-1584)

CATHERINE THE GREAT
(1683-1727)

STEREO 'SCARFACE' LAMBRETTA
(1451-1503)

BEPPO THE NAUGHTY
(1462-1573)

THE MARQUIS OF EGG
(1554-1597)

FIELD MARSHALL
'BOFFER' ROBERTS
(1782-1846)

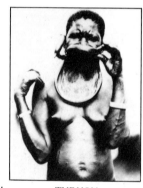

THE HON.
NELLY EVERSHED-ROPER
(1811-1894)

HER SUBLIME HIGHNESS CAROL
AURORA THATCHER,
Twin to the Honourable Mark.

*An Urcheon Per Party A Cleavage Displayed
Enhanced Between Two Earmuffs, A Coat Sable
Pendant. Motto: "Keep Smiling".*

HER SERENE HIGHNESS
MARGARET HILDA THATCHER,
PVC
Leader of the Realm, Commander-in-Chief of the
Armed Forces, Ruler of England, Scotland, Wales,
the Falkland Isles and Parts of Northern Ireland.

*Sinister Chief A Cat-A-Mountain Proper Affronte
Embattled in a Field of Fylfots and Mannikins
Subservient. Motto: "Do not Interrupt".*

A GENEALO

'IRONHEAD' THATCHER
(1873-1928)

GWENDOLENE VON OFTERDINGEN
(5,000,765-5,000,693 BC)

OSWALD DE CATFORD
(4,656-4,595 BC)

LADY FLORENCE PIGGE
(4,703-4,622 BC)

CAIUS CAESAR (CALIGULA)
(13-41 AD)

PUNTER'S FANCY
(10-1)

CONFUCIUS
(551-479 BC)

GERAINT PILBEAM
(1671-1746)

DONALD DUCK
(1823-1894)

GLORIA WALLABY
(1893-1959)

GERALD 'SONNY' THATCHER
(1885-1948)

LORD PRUNEHAT DE THATCHER
(1641-1710)

JOAN OF GLASGOW
(1655-1715)

HIS GRACE DENIS NORMAN
ALBERT PAUNCEFOOT
MASSINGBIRD DESIREE
THATCHER, AA, RAC,

Duke of Connaught, Marquess of Granby, Queen's
Head and Eight Bells, Muriel's Afternoon Drinking
Club, Prince Consort.

*Two Legs Akimbo A Flask Graspant on a Right
Bender Supported in Arms by Two Bluff Serjeants of
Wavy Azure, Thereon a Chapeau Trilby. Motto:
"Hic Pardon".*

THE HONOURABLE MARK
ABELARD DE GRISBY THATCHER,
Chairman and Managing Director of Monteagle
Securities, Reliable Banking Services of Bahrein
Ltd, Heir Apparent.

*A Sloth at Gaze Repugnant, Thereon an Open Hand
Engreased with the Fees, a Pale Face Vert Pukant.
Motto: "Mater will Pay".*

AL TABLE

AMONG OUR SOUVENIRS...

The celebration of these fifty glorious years has been, I am glad to say, yet another spur to urge on the unemployed to find themselves a job. Though much of the merchandise available on the occasion is in fact cobbled together by the Korean and the Jap, these ladies on the right are seen enjoying the work of unpacking it. This unpacking of Japanese souvenirs is a very ancient craft and has been passed down from mother to daughter in this particular unpacking plant for many generations.

Any celebration, be it the celebration of a glorious jubilee, of a victory on land, sea or on the rugby football ground, or merely an opportunity to get plastered for the sheer fun of it, will produce spontaneous works of art. It may be an extempore poem or limerick that will make the rafters of the snug bar ring with merry laughter for hours afterwards. It may be some manifestation of what is now I believe called 'performance art' – a collection of red lights, belisha beacons and park benches surmounted by a policeman's helmet. Whatever it is, it provides great satisfaction to those who make it, and forms a delightful memento of the occasion. In the picture on the left my wife is seen fondling just such a memento, in the form of a small statuette of herself as Diana the Huntress, a fairly terrifying woman in the mercifully remote past who pursued brother fox across the hills and dales of ancient Greece. The woman on the left is seen looking on with evident admiration and respect.

Artistic criticism is a very valuable part of the creative process. In my picture on the right an art lover is seen engaged in an aesthetic discussion with a gallery owner as to the merits or demerits of a small plaster bust of my wife, Margaret Hilda Thatcher.

STREET PARTIES

A GOOD TIME IS HAD BY ALL: CELEBRATIONS IN PROGRESS IN SOUTH LONDON TO MARK CUTS IN PERSONAL INCOME TAX FOR THOSE EARNING MORE THAN £100,000 A YEAR.

My wife, Margaret Hilda Thatcher, has always aroused very passionate feelings, not only in the hearts of visiting Arab potentates, but also in the bosoms of her own people, whether they be decent ordinary folk or members of the so-called working classes. Their enthusiasm has spilled over, again and again, in the spontaneous 'street parties' that have so often been thrown – with a great deal else besides – to mark the high points of her long and very glorious reign. Whether it be brother fuzzy-wuzzy dancing round a fire in Brixton or some squat, bow-legged and physically unappealing scouse 'git' lobbing half a brick at the constabulary in Toxteth, it is hard to picture a more heartwarming and often indeed handwarming display of *joie de vivre*. It is easy enough for their betters to sneer: for the more sophisticated a champagne bottle thrown through a stained glass window, the thrill of releasing the handbrake on a friend's new Rolls-Royce and watching it roll smoothly over a cliff, the sheer fun of poking an oar through a Rembrandt may seem the only ways to enjoy oneself. But hats off to these simpler souls who can have a perfectly

agreeable time with nothing more elaborate than a petrol can and a box of matches.

With the blessings of unemployment more widely distributed, golf clubs, striptease parlours and afternoon drinking establishments are increasingly under pressure to admit the unsuitable. How much better, therefore, that they should be 'out on the streets' making merry in their own way. 'Letting off steam' is only natural, and the bobby on the beat with time on his hands is always ready to join in the fun. On a more practical level, these street parties have been of immense benefit in solving the problem of the inner cities. Even the most enthusiastic devotees of a more slimline economy would hesitate to plough up a flourishing high street in order to grow potatoes or turnips. A thorough crop-burning operation by friend yobbo, on the other hand, not only clears the site with immense savings in demolition costs, havering by wishy-washy conservationists, etc, but lays down a fertile topsoil of ash.

MAKING THINGS GO WITH A BANG. A SPONTANEOUS EXPLOSION OF ENTHUSIASM IN THE TOXTETH AREA OF LIVERPOOL AT GOVERNMENT SCHEMES TO ALLOW OPEN-CAST COALMINING IN THE CITY CENTRE.

We are often accused, as a nation, of being too tight-lipped and buttoned-up. Hoorah for these brave British hooligans, however muddled they may be in their political thinking, for giving us once again a reputation abroad for doing it best when it comes to 'making whoopee'.

BOYS WILL BE BOYS: UNEMPLOYED YOUTHS JOIN IN THE FUN WITH A VENGEANCE AS REVELRY REIGNS SUPREME. GALA NIGHT IN THE NORTH-EAST.

THE MARGARET HILDA THATCHER MONUMENT

The task of creating a colossal monument on a scale worthy of my wife Margaret's own true stature both at home and overseas has been a daunting one to the run of monumental masons. The process of chipping a likeness out of the living rock, be it granite or some more durable substance, is a slow one, and my wife Our Leader is never one to waste time. Many a time indeed and oft she has grown impatient and made her departure even before the diminutive figure in beret and smock, dwarfed to near insignificance by the mass of unhewn stone, has reached the top of the ladder and turned to lift a thumb.

Nonetheless, some tribute on this gigantic scale is clearly called for, and after necessary test work with barrage balloon maquettes, I am glad to say that several supertankers are even now on the high seas transporting many thousand tons of fine British-quarried Carrara marble to the Falkland Islands. Here work has already begun on this vast erection. When completed it will be clearly visible from Buenos Aires, showing Margaret in the guise of a defiant Britannia brandishing a handbag at the mainland, straddling the harbour at Port Stanley, and fitted with aircraft warning lights.

AN UNSATISFACTORY FIRST ATTEMPT: A STATUE OF MY WIFE OUR LEADER COMMISSIONED FROM THE SCULPTOR MANUEL PRATTFACE TO STAND IN THE GENTLEMENS' WASHROOM AT THE CARLTON SENIOR CITIZENS' CLUB. COMPLETED IN MARGARET'S UNAVOIDABLE ABSENCE, IT WAS FELT BY CRITICS TO BE 'TOO EFFEMINATE'.

EMPLOYMENT FOR THE 'SHEEPSHAGGERS' OF PORT STANLEY: THE ENTIRE MALE POPULATION OF THE BRITISH FALKLAND ISLANDS GATHERS TO LEND A HAND IN ASSEMBLING BRITISH BORN SCULPTOR MAURICE BANGOLD'S COLOSSAL STATUE OF MY WIFE. INSET: A SCALE MODEL OF THE FALKLANDS COLOSSUS.

WORLD LEADERS UNITE TO PAY HOMAGE

There is, it seems, no corner of the inhabited globe where my wife's name does not immediately provoke a response. As will be seen from these goodwill messages from world leaders, she enjoys a respect and esteem on the international stage unequalled since the days of the Emperor Napoleon.

HRH THE MORON OF TWAT
In the night watches you come to me in dreams, Woman of Perfection. Many a time and oft I have awoken, shouting your precious name to the purple vault of Heaven. Empress! What music we could make together, you and I!

COLONEL GADDAFI
Your destabilisation of neighbouring regimes, not least among them the European Community, the British Labour Party and the Democratic Peoples' Socialist Republic of the Falkland Islands, your use of crack hit squads and readiness to override the craven mutterings of elected peoples' committees make you my heroine. Gorillas all over the world raise their hand in a fraternal salute.

GENERAL MING OF THE RIGHT WING INTERGALACTIC FRONT
Woman of Iron, your power is so pathetically limited! With your practical housewifely policies, inherited from your esteemed forbear 'Economical' Alf, and my megatron laser universectomy apparatus we could make the cosmos more competitive in a twinkling.

HIS EXCELLENCY PRESIDENT FILTHISWEIN OF CARAMBA
My visit to your esteemed realm, triumph that it was over the decadent liberal shirtlifters at odds with my internal law and order policies, remains a memory I and my junta of strong women will always treasure. Hoorah for the thwack of firm government, Margaret Hilda!

THE ADMINISTRATIVE COUNCIL, PORT STANLEY
Like many 'gay' groups, we have over the years been the victim of callous 'sheepist' attacks, suggesting in some cases that relations between sheep and consenting adult human beings might raise eyebrows and much else besides. Thank you, Margaret Hilda, for your generous allocation of public moneys from the UK to provide a suitable venue where we can pursue our chosen bent unmolested.

ROYAL BOROUGH OF KENSINGTON AND CHELSEA ARTS COMMITTEE
Ta very much, Doll. A kind of liberty is what it's all about in our view and that is what we intend to take. Be good, and if you can't be good be careful.

AUBERON 'FOUR-EYES' DEMPSTER-WAUGH, PRESIDENT ELECT, 1922 COMMITTEE
Monsters say you're the Greatest, Right? Okay.

Johnnie Consort

Bored out of his mind but still going strong...

In his unique position as consort to Our Leader Margaret Hilda Thatcher, her husband Denis has his ear very close to the seat of power, and in addition to unequalled access to people of influence, enjoys the advantage of ample leisure. He is available for after-dinner speaking, opening ceremonies at licensed premises, and for a small number of directorships. Why not ring 01 – if you're outside London – 222 9000 (8 lines) and ask to speak to Mr Picarda in Bookings.

GI'S A JOB

BEHIND THE SCENES

Presenting the Leader and her enlightened policies to the nation and the world is the privilege of the mammoth Saatchi & Saatchi organisation.

No detail is left to chance: spontaneous political demonstration, off-the-cuff interview with the press at London airport, or unscheduled walkabout in an Ulster shopping precinct, every second has to be scripted, story-boarded, rehearsed and recorded.

"*Intolerance, Gone with the Wind, Tweetie Pie's Funny Christmas Party* – forget them! This is epic!" says Saatchis' Director Herkules von Blofeld. "We're not making movies, we're making history!"

Margate Sands provide the convincing backdrop for Margaret Hilda Thatcher's visit to Jordan in this *News at Ten* coverage of the trip.

A 'Wet' receives instruction.

THE ROLE OF THE WHIPS

With the best will in the world, not even leading Tory politicians can always grasp the subtleties of the Leader's policies at first sight. From time to time they inevitably fail to understand some finer point.

It is then the task of the so-called 'Whips' to explain and to clarify.

Using the most sophisticated audio-visual equipment, the Whips set out to bring home the real meaning of Conservative policy – squeeze, cut or merely the smack of tough government – in a way they will take in, introducing them as it were step by step to an understanding of their duties and responsibilities.

'Whips' see themselves, rightly, as the spiritual elite of the Tory Party: Father Confessors charged by Our Leader to keep pure the spirit of acquisitiveness and self-interest that lie at the core of Tory thinking.

THE POLLSTERS

Head of Our Leader's Prediction Research Information Centre at Kettering, Sir Laurens van der Post sifts information on future events.

To be able to predict with accuracy the most subtle shifts in public opinion is a vital part of the task of sustaining Our Leader's power. Only with accurate advance information is it possible to pre-empt and forestall the forces of disorder and others wishing to destabilize Our Leader's regime.

Led by Margaret Hilda Thatcher's own personal spirit guide, Sir Laurens van der Post, the backroom boys responsible for this work are on a twenty-four-hours round-the-clock standby, working in shifts to study and co-ordinate data about the future as it comes in.

As soon as the first indications are received, they are analysed by experts and then passed to Headquarters in the Saatchi building for immediate action. Troops or police go tumbling into the streets, television and radio stations are put on red alert, and the necessary declarations of war or emergency brought to the Leader for signature.

A team of analysts at Tory Central Office awaits news of Our Leader Margaret Hilda Thatcher's future policies.

Gordon Reece: His patient honing produced the voice to which the nation thrills. He compares the minute adjustments to pitch and tone to tuning a great engine in the pits, or a slide trombone. He is seen here relaxing after a hard day in the Acoustibooth, playing a round on his private golf course in Santa Monica.

"Mr Wonderful"

Ask who it is who coached Our Leader through the years of experiment and research that finally produced 'that voice'.

For some there is something in that cello-smooth timbre that would indicate the legacy of Sergeant Major Brittan of the Guards. Others believe they can detect a hint of Louis Armstrong or the 'Puddytat Sylvester' of Mel Blanc.

True, Margaret Hilda Thatcher did study voice production with Lord Olivier, and there may, in private moments, be a faint echo of his Richard the Third, with its unpredictable swoops and sudden leaps into falsetto.

But the slow, perfectly controlled baritone of lengthened vowels and heart-stopping sincerity that has etched itself as with a gramophone needle on the listening eardrums of her people is the work of one man – Gordon Reece.

'Wee Gordon' – he is little over two foot six in height – owes his expertise to years of training as a comedy producer at Lord Grade's Associated Television.

"It's all really in the timing, isn't it?" he muses today, struggling with the stubborn cork of a champagne bottle almost bigger than he is. "True in LE – Light Entertainment – true in sex, sport, politics, life. You name it, timing is" – a sudden crack and champagne erupts in a gusher of foaming white bubbles to drench his handmade blue dinner suit – "everything. Have some shampoo

How did he begin, this patriotic Professor Higgins i miniature, now living, for sentimental reasons, withi sight of the rolling Pacific, in the United States o America? I put the question, tentatively, over *Crêpes d Chine au Calamité* he has whisked into existence with hi own fair hands in his penthouse *bachelière* in Los Angeles

Gordon Reece clasps those same small but perfec hands and wriggles vole-like among the cushions.

"One began by being overwhelmed by the shee potential of the thing. Here was this instrument, thi secret weapon if you like, that could destroy al competition, smash plate glass at fifty miles, reduc strong men to tears, knock out intercontinental ballisti missiles, blow people's minds. And yet it wasn't working.'

"All it needed was a tweak here and a tweak there, a bi taken out at the top end and a bit put back at the botton end, and we'd be in business. It was so daunting. Little me, able to lift one finger and release all that terrifyin power, maybe change the course of history. Then realised I was unable to stop myself. It was like standing i a garage and knowing one was in the presence of som mechanical monster that was only waiting for me to fiddl with its sparking plugs to roar into life and amaze th world. I just had to get underneath and start muckin about."

"A talent to amaze..."

To meet 'The Master' at home in his Belgravia Studio, to sit with him as his long pale fingers ramble over the keys of his white Bechstein, is to be astonished by the modesty of the man. To watch as the lightly-powdered lids half-closed in ecstacy at some utterly original chord stroked from the ivories, to see the white smoke drift up from the long, long cigarette holder clenched between those white, white teeth, you might think you were in the presence of a mere entertainer. Only when he stops playing, takes the cigarette holder and cradles it between those sensitive hands, shrugging his shantung dressing gown about him, and begins to speak, so beautifully that his parrot Mr Puff swings suddenly upside down on his perch and says "Crikey", do we realise we are in the presence of genius.

"Where there is harmony, may we bring discord" – "U-turn if you want to, the lady's not for turning!" – "Rejoice!" – If the Leader says it, he has written it.

'Ronnie', now 'Sir Ronnie' Millar, is still "a teensy bit baffled" by the miraculous recognition of his powers in middle life, the transformation from humble scriptwriter, adapter of the works of C.P. Snow for the West End stage, to the Shakespeare of our day, a man whose words are graven already on the wall of history, chiselled in stone, immortal.

"Call it the magic of Madam." He takes a tiny puff at the ivory mouthpiece of that famous Fabergé holder, and

'Sir Ronnie' Millar, the Leader's scriptwriter. As author of the *Prayer of St. Francis of Assisi*, and Margaret Hilda's 'U-turn if you want to' speech, 'Sir Ronnie' already enjoys the longest entry in the *Guinness Book Of Records*, as responsible for more literary quotations than Shakespeare and the *Bible* combined.

contemplates the three inches of perfect ash on the end of his cigarette. "There I was, sitting in the stalls of some frightful flea-pit, listening to my words being mangled and mauled by one terrible little actress after another – no style, no panache, not a television camera in sight – and then Shazam!!! One heard one's words enunciated for the first time as they were written to be enunciated: sung, rendered, whammed for six across the footlights. And not to five or six grisly old ladies in hearing aids littered about the stalls like a mild attack of measles, but to billions of people. Coast to coast. It was orgasmic."

'Sir Ronnie' Millar (l) and Margaret Hilda Thatcher (r) at Number Ten,
put the finishing touches to a speech on the miners' strike.

Putting on a good face

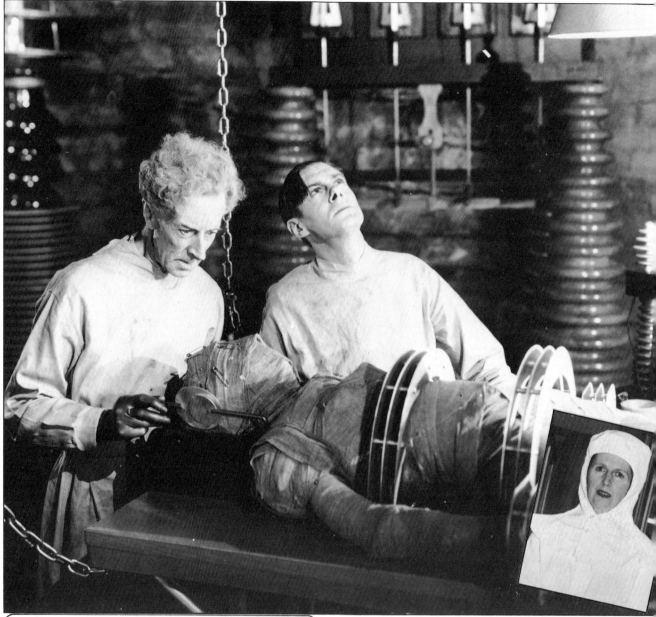

Speed is of the essence: during a five minute break in delicate EEC negotiations in Brussels, HSH Margaret Hilda Thatcher is given a skin-toning vibra-therapy treatment by team leader Dr Foster (l) and his assistant Dr Stonehouse.

Crowds the world over have marvelled at the clear complexion and flawless beauty of Our Leader Margaret Hilda Thatcher. However gruelling the schedule, however taxing the negotiations, Margaret Hilda Thatcher's poise remains unruffled, her freshness unsullied.

Like every other facet of Our Leader's Achievement, this is a hard-won victory. Waiting 'off-stage', whether at an international conference, summit meeting between world leaders, or a local Young Conservative dance, a highly-trained team of handpicked beauticians, skin specialists, pore cleansers, tissue rejuvenators and gay hairdressers is standing by. Like mechanics in the pits in her earlier days, they know they have only micro-seconds at their disposal to strip the Leader down, carry out essential checks, and make the necessary 'running repairs' before Margaret Hilda Thatcher is back on the road,

facing the cameras, out under the lights, trading insult with Monsieur Mitterand or yelling blue murder at Mr Ghandi.

Leader of the team, Dr Foster, ridicules suggestion that his work could be carried out within the National Health Service. Nevertheless he sees it as a typical instance of private medicine producing useful 'spin-off' that may later be of general use to NHS patients.

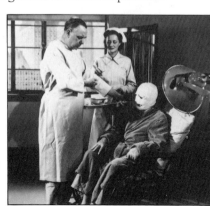

Repairing the ravages: Consort Denis Thatcher is wheeled into the treatment area after gruelling hours on the platform at Conservative Party Conference.